SIMON & SCHUSTER BOOKS FOR YOUNG READERS
Simon & Schuster Building, Rockefeller Center, 1230 Avenue of
the Americas, New York, New York 10020. Copyright © 1991 by
Hachette, France, and The Cousteau Society, Inc. English translation
copyright © 1992 by The Cousteau Society, Inc. All rights reserved
including the right of reproduction in whole or in part in any form.
Originally published in France by Hachette Jeunesse as LES SECRETS
DES ANTIPODES. SIMON & SCHUSTER BOOKS FOR YOUNG READERS is a
trademark of Simon & Schuster. Manufactured in Italy. 10 9 8 7 6
5 4 3 2 1

CREDITS
THE COUSTEAU SOCIETY, Captain Jacques-Yves Cousteau,
Jean-Michel Cousteau, Project Director: Pamela Stacey, Author: Paula
DiPerna, Photo Editor: Judy K. Brody, Research: Christine Causse,
Design Consultant: André Demaison, Photographers: Richard C.
Murphy: 6–7, 8, 9, 10, 12, 16, 21, 24, 27, 32–40, 45, Anne-Marie
Cousteau: 21, 25, 26, 28, 43, 44, Didier Noirot: 13, 17, 19, 24, 28, 29,
41, 44, Norbert Wu: cover, 3, 10, 11, 12, 14–15, 17, 18, 30, 33, 36,
François Sarano: 16, 21, 22–23, 30–31, 31, 42, Roger V. Grace: 32, 37,
Veronique Sarano-Simon: 20, Philippe Lemasson: 4–5, Graphic
Design: Carmèle Delivré and François Huertas.

Library of Congress Cataloging-in-Publication Data
New Zealand / the Cousteau Society.   p.   cm.   Summary: A brief
introduction to Maori culture, indigenous plants and animals and
natural sites of New Zealand.   1. New Zealand—Description and
travel—1981– —Juvenile literature.   2. Natural history—New
Zealand—Juvenile literature.   [1. New Zealand—Description and
travel.   2. Natural history—New Zealand.]   I. Cousteau Society.
DU413.N32   1992   993—dc20   91-32922   CIP
ISBN: 0-671-77072-1

The Cousteau Society

AN ADVENTURE IN
NEW ZEALAND

SIMON & SCHUSTER BOOKS FOR YOUNG READERS
Published by Simon & Schuster
New York • London • Toronto • Sydney • Tokyo • Singapore

WELCOME

"Harae mai, harae mai, harae mai." "Welcome, welcome, welcome." So chant the Maori to make visitors feel at home, including the Cousteau team embarked on a new expedition. The Maori, the first people to settle in New Zealand, are Polynesians who traveled in very large canoes, sometimes for days and months, stopping at one place and then another until they finally reached New Zealand about a thousand years ago. Some Maori legends tell of a first leader who rode to New Zealand on the back of a whale.

The Maori used the fibers of the flax plant, weaving over 200 strands, to make a skirt.

The haka, a warrior's dance, is meant to display strength to visitors.

In a far corner of the world, the Maori welcome the Cousteau team by dancing a haka.

A challenger tests newcomers to see if they are enemies, but never really means to fight.

Dutch, French and English expeditions explored the Pacific Ocean in the 18th century, searching for new lands and unknown territories. Until they arrived in New Zealand they had no idea Maori society existed. Today's New Zealand is a crossroads of many different cultures. About three million people from all over the world now live here, and many learn Maori customs, music and language. Young and old sometimes try out the canoe paddle on holidays or when special guests are honored.

A hundred rowers could fit in a canoe carved from one enormous tree.

At the end of the welcome, hosts and guests rub noses to signify the mixing of their breath. According to Maori belief, this exchange recreates the breath of the world, possible only between true friends.

A Maori leader rests after
the ceremony.

Maori wood sculpture records important events and fantastic creatures.

A Maori canoe greets *Calypso*, trailing streamers that legend says are resting places for spirits of the wind and ocean.

The Maori have no written language, so they carve their history in wood. A wooden mask is like a photograph of a person, and canoes are decorated with the faces of ancestors or leaders so they will not be forgotten. Tall posts are truly a family tree of portraits of parents, grandparents, great-grandparents—as far back as anyone knows.

Maori meeting houses are sometimes carved with creatures climbing toward the sky.

The glistening eyes of masks are made of shiny abalone shell, called paua.

After meeting the Maori, the Cousteau team begins to explore the fiery heart of New Zealand.

Calypso's helicopter, Felix, hovers near the cone of White Island, an active volcano where the heat on land could sometimes melt the helicopter's floats.

THE SMOKING EARTH

The crew doesn't get too close to a steaming pool where the water is hot enough to brew tea.

New Zealand is geologically young compared to other places—only about a million years old. The land remains restless with many live volcanoes and lingering volcanic action. Smoke fumes and hisses through cracks in the earth.

In volcanic zones, pressure builds on underground gases forcing them to escape. In the area of Rotorua, this hot energy underground is captured in pipes to heat homes or generate electricity in a geo-thermal plant.

Geysers erupt at intervals in volcanic zones, spraying hot water and steam.

Hundreds of hot springs and geysers occur in the Rotorua area. A geyser works like a fizzy bottle of soda—gases trapped underground push to be released and force hot water jets into the air.

In New Zealand, the land not only smokes, but also boils and bubbles.

Lava fires and ash smothered the forest that once grew at White Island.

Even clay and rock melt if temperatures are high enough. Hot mud pools can be heard as well as seen in New Zealand's geothermal area, plopping and gurgling, they sound like something cooking on a stove. In fact some pools are named "porridge pot" and "jumping frogs." A splash from the mud can cause a bad burn. But new shapes and colors of mud are born with each thump and bubble. And in the hot springs, sulphur and other minerals build stony terraces with rainbow-colored crusts.

The temperature of the mud can reach over 190°F.

Hot spring water flows over rocks or near lakes.

In the fjord region, tumbling waterfalls thunder into the ocean.

Fjordland is one of the wettest places on earth. Here, rain falls constantly and sometimes cloud and mist mix with rushing white water spray. Once there was so much wet fog that *Calypso*'s helicopter pilot could not tell where the sky ended and the sea began.

The fjords are giant bays along the coast, and deep green forests cover the land that juts into the sea. When rain washes from the woods onto the ocean surface, the freshwater floats on top since it is less dense than saltwater. The fjords were clawed out by glaciers —rivers of slow-moving ice that scraped through this area about 15,000 years ago.

In Fjordland the team found tough and magnificent terrain and hideaway corners where few people have ever stepped foot.

Even water takes on strange forms here.

Hot water about 122°F rises to a surface pool and glistens with gas bubbles.

Franz Josef glacier is a tongue of ice flowing between rough mountains and steamy rain forest.

In Auckland Island, a small island in the coldest part of New Zealand, wild blowing winds keep a waterfall from falling.

A UNIQUE WORLD

Some rata trees grow in thick forests that have never been cut

The crew treks to a cave deep in the 'tangled bush.

The trees in some places are so packed together they seem like a solid dome. The rata tree has red flowers, and beneath the blossoms, there is a busy community of plants. New Zealanders call their woods "the bush" and they are very proud of it. Eighty-four percent of the plants found here do not exist anywhere else in the world. The bush grows in canopies

The forests of Fjordland seemed
velvety to the touch.

Some ferns in New Zealand are descendants of prehistoric plants.

with very tall trees standing over
smaller ones. The smallest trees in
turn stand over younger shrubs
and seedlings, which in turn stand
over carpets of spongy moss.
Climbing plants creep from one
level to another and epiphytes,
plants that live on others, perch
everywhere. Whatever you touch
feels soft—there are no thorns
and stickers.

Feathery umbrella ferns can grow to 30 feet
tall, shading the forest floor below.

The yellow-eyed penguin is the rarest penguin in the world. The Maori call it "hoiho" for the calling sound it makes. Living on crab, fish and other food from the sea, this penguin needs a bushy sheltered shoreline in which to nest. The penguin lays its eggs in thick grass and hops over branches and tree roots to come and go from the ocean. When trees are cut along the coast, the penguins have less space to breed. Without their forest protection, penguin colonies can get smaller because there is no safe place to lay an egg.

Forests are so important as shelter that even mother sea lions use them. They have their babies deep in the woods, or haul them under the branches out of the wind and far from the raging waves of ocean storms.

The yellow-eyed penguin lives only in New Zealand. While parents are out fishing to feed them, the young stay on land, trying their wings, although penguins don't fly.

The forests are so welcoming that even sea creatures come there to rest and rear their young.

A young yellow-eyed penguin still wears a helmet of baby feathers.

26

The hooker sea lion also lives only in New Zealand and families scatter through the woods at Auckland Island during the season when pups are born.

The odd kiwi bird is the symbol of New Zealand.

Kiwis live in deep tough grass, travel only at night and cannot fly.

Crew members watch a mother takahe feed its baby.

A wounded kiwi is nursed back to health at a "hospital" especially for kiwi birds.

Because New Zealand is so far from any other land, many animals that lived elsewhere in the world could not travel the distance. So New Zealand has no native mammals and no snakes. Without such natural predators, unique birds developed. These birds did not have to escape creatures on the ground, and they evolved without real wings since they had no need to fly.

Of these flightless birds, the

At last reaching the cave, the team reassembles the skeleton of a moa leg.

Protections came too late for the moa, a gigantic ostrich-like bird that could not fly. The toothless moa survived on twigs, tough grass and seeds and swallowed rocks to help it digest. Easily spotted in the bush, the moa became an inviting target for early hunters, who ate its meat and used its skin for feathered cloaks. Today no moas exist.

The moa was the largest bird ever to live. It stood about 12 feet tall.

kiwi is the most famous. Seeing poorly, it uses its long beak like a walking stick to sniff out insects and worms and dig them from their hiding places to eat.

But human settlers brought animals to New Zealand that meant trouble for the grounded birds. Rats hitched rides on boats; deer were introduced for sport hunting; sheep were brought to begin the meat and wool industries. These new animals either chased the birds or trampled the bush in which the birds lived. Little by little, the flightless birds began to disappear.

One bird, the takahe, was thought to be extinct. But in 1948 a very small colony was located in a remote lonely valley where no animals or humans had ever been. Today, New Zealand operates a center where takahe eggs and young hatched birds are protected before being released to the wild.

Elephant fish usually live in very deep water at 1300–1800 feet, and must come to shallow waters to lay their eggs.

The elephant fish resembles a weird undersea airplane. Its skin seems like a silvery crinkling cloth. With its long snout, the fish feels out its direction, patting along the bottom in the murky water. Usually living in the deepest, darkest parts of the ocean, the elephant fish didn't seem to like the camera lights. The crew stayed just long enough to take a few pictures, since almost no one has ever seen an elephant fish underwater.

Even though some birds don't fly, some fish do!

A relative of the shark, the elephant fish lays its eggs in yellowish capsules, two at a time. Unfortunately boats in the fish-and-chips industry lay miles of net to catch elephant fish just at egg-laying season. Some fish are caught before they can hatch any young, so in the future, there may be fewer of these bizarre creatures.

What look giant elephant ears are the fins that propel the fish.

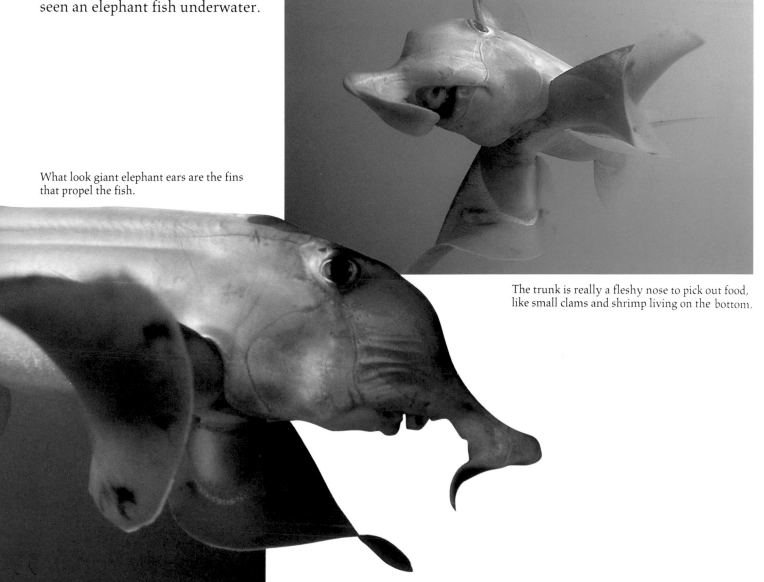

The trunk is really a fleshy nose to pick out food, like small clams and shrimp living on the bottom.

In the Kermadec Islands, regulations protect groupers from spear guns and hooks. These fish can grow to be several feet long and when seen from some angles make a diver look small.

In such clear water, some animals look like plants,
some plants look like feathers.

Sea anemone tentacles surround their mouth.

The tentacles of the anemone capture the animal's food.

This animal, a bryozoa, drapes like a mossy plant.

A sea anemone seen very close.

Fishing earns a lot of money for the economy of New Zealand. But in some places, no fishing or disruption of any kind is permitted. And in protected waters, we find a diverse carpet of living things.

Brilliantly colored creatures exist together, folding and bursting like stars. Sea anemones are animals named for flowers, but the arms that look like petals contain darts the creature uses to harpoon food like fish, crabs and other small swimmers and crawlers. The anemone snares its prey, stings it with venom, then swoops it into its waiting mouth.

Algae (the delicate plumes on the far right), are plants of the sea. Sea plants are necessary to use energy from the sun to make food for sea animals. Also, some fish perch on algae branches, like birds on trees. Other fish graze on algae like sheep in a New Zealand meadow.

In a healthy clean ocean, living things need nothing special to survive except each other.

The brilliant-colored nudibranch is a snail without a shell!

Sliding along on a foot under its body, the nudibranch moves slowly through the sea. A shell-less snail, it breathes through the tube-like gills on its back. Nudibranchs eat creatures that have a bad taste—like anemones and sponges. This is a form of defense—by eating what tastes bad, the nudibranch tastes bad too, so no creature wants to eat it. The bright colors and spots warn other creatures away, like a red light that says "don't eat me."

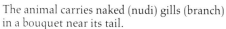
The animal carries naked (nudi) gills (branch) in a bouquet near its tail.

It slithers along using two antennae to smell for food and a mate.

Nudibranchs slink along alone on stems of seaweed or mate with each other in the shallow water.

Two nudibranchs turn slowly in a spiral to mate and lay a perfect swirl of tiny eggs.

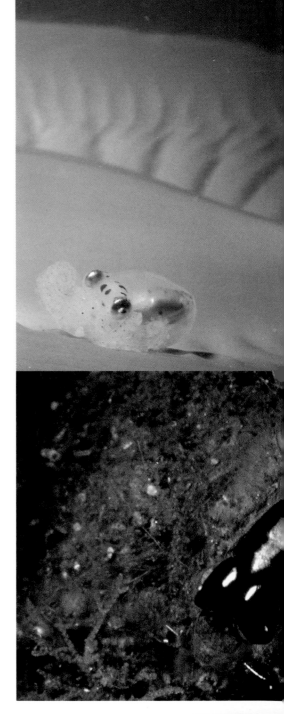

A transparent baby octopus can barely be seen against the egg case of an elephant fish.

The sea is rich in hiding places and hiding faces. Camouflage keeps many creatures from being found and eaten by a larger creature, or helps them stalk prey without being seen. Some sea animals can change colors like chameleons to match the background. The large groupers the crew encountered in New Zealand could change from solid gray to speckled to silvery stripes in seconds. Some fishes look like rocks or seaweed. The scorpion fish blends in perfectly on the seafloor. It waits there, staying still until a meal comes along. Then the fish just opens its jaws wide and sucks in its prey.

The flexible boneless baby octopus can bend into very tight corners to hide. Some creatures, like the delicate comb jelly, are transparent and nearly invisible. The comb jelly can only be seen when the diver's light shines through its watery body, as on the next page where it seems like a spaceship gliding near the sun.

Camouflage protects both hunter and hunted.

A scorpion fish hides among a bed of anemones.

A tiny fish rests near the curving arm of a starfish.

An eel conceals itself in a bundle of coral.

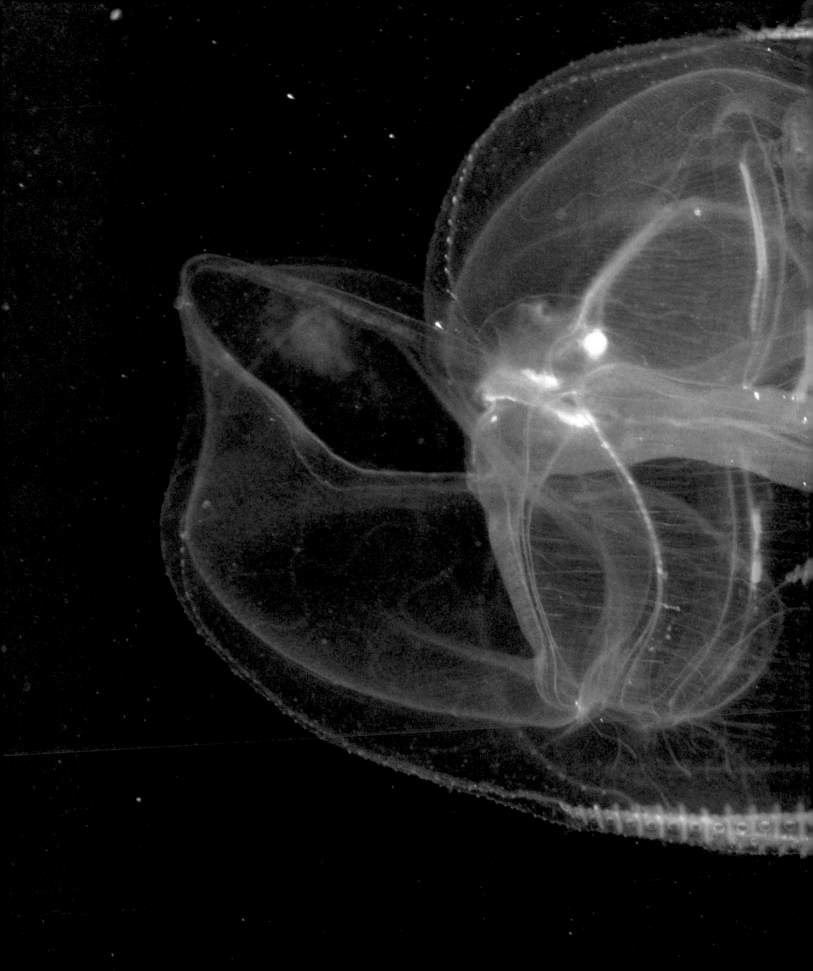

Each arm of this ship is a fishing pole with many, many hooks.

A NEW CHALLENGE

Calypso came upon a fleet of giant squid fishing boats lit up in the night. They looked like floating factories designed to catch as many squid as possible. The New Zealand government sets limits on how many squid each boat can catch, but patrolling the ocean to enforce the rules is not easy. People eat squid, but so do penguins and seals. Some scientists worry that if humans catch too many squid, there won't be enough left for ocean creatures looking for food.

Sometimes even good intentions can cause bad results. In 1865, humans brought goats to the far-away Auckland Islands so the animals could be hunted for food in case survivors from shipwrecks washed ashore. But today there are too many goats, all hungry, eating and destroying too many plants. A New Zealand Navy ship helped in a rescue program, carrying some goats away so the grasses could grow back.

The team helped capture wild goats that were destroying unusual plants.

New Zealand tries to find the right balance between modern living and respect for the environment.

Even large modern cities are infused with the
traditions of the past.

Wellington, New Zealand's capital is a modern city situated on a natural harbor.

New Zealand is very far from all other countries. Yet, New Zealanders live a good life because they have fish, wood and farm products to trade, and unusual surroundings to enjoy.

The Maori people believe much can be learned from their ancestors about how to respect the land and wisely use what it can provide. But all New Zealanders must share in the resources and the decisions. Like other nations, New Zealand must choose between how much to exploit and how much to safeguard for the future.

The *Calypso* crew receives the gift of a hand-carved Maori canoe paddle.

A group of young Maori construct a canoe similar to the vessels that carried their ancestors to New Zealand.

In the legends of New Zealand, the white heron means good luck. Like the people of New Zealand, the heron came from other lands, blown across the oceans by the wind. The heron nests in colonies, but is not seen very often. So the flight of a heron can signal great events ahead.

Using the tools of his ancestors, a young Maori carves the prow of a new canoe, spending weeks to perfect each notch and cut.

The jagged islands of New Zealand lie like puzzle pieces in the sea. *Calypso* navigated around all the coasts, in and out of many bays, from the coldest point in the south to the warmest in the north. In a land as alone as a castaway sailor, *Calypso* found the challenges of today as well as the dreams of tomorrow.

KERMADEC ISLANDS

NORTH ISLAND

Whangarei

Aukland

WHITE ISLAND

BAY OF PLENTY

Tauranga

Rotorua

Gisborne

New Plymouth

Hastings

Wanganui

TASMAN SEA

Wellington

Nelson

Franz Josef Glacier

PACIFIC OCEAN

Christchurch

SOUTH ISLAND

Fjordland

Dunedin

STEWART ISLAND

AUKLAND ISLANDS

NEW ZEALAND VITAL STATISTICS

Area: 103,736 square miles, including all outer islands (about the same size as Japan or the British Isles)

Population: March 31, 1990: 3.3504 million (official estimate of Department of Statistics, New Zealand)

Largest Cities: Auckland, Christchurch, Wellington, Hamilton, Dunedin

Principal Exports: Meat (especially lamb and mutton), dairy products, wool, forest products, agricultural products, fish

Approximately 1000 miles long, but only about 300 miles wide; length of coastline, approximately 3500 miles.

Country spans from sub-tropical waters in the north (warm) to sub-Antarctic waters in the south (cold).

Each geographical feature (mountain, lake, etc.) has both a Maori name and an English name and often both are officially recognized.

The Maori name for New Zealand is "Aotearoa," meaning The Land of the Long White Cloud.